A Serious Guide to Starting Your Own Business

Peter K. Black

Copyright © 2014 Pierre Jereczek

All rights reserved

To all my readers an my wonderful wife

Table of content:

Introduction

Chapter One: Coming up with your Idea

Chapter Two: Building your Business Plan

Chapter Three: Choosing your Business Structure

Chapter Four: Finding your Businesses location

Chapter Five: Getting your Dream Financed

Chapter Six: Hiring your Employees

Chapter Seven: Location, Location, Location

Chapter Eight: Opening day

Chapter Nine: After the celebration has ended

Conclusion

INTRODUCTION

When you are in the process of starting your own business, there are a lot of things that you should and should not do to get the best results for your efforts. This can be a very exciting and yet in a lot of regards stressful time for a person to go through. All of the arrangements that need to be made along with taking the time to make sure that you have covered every step along the way. All that you have to look at, it is understandable that you may forget a thing or two along the way. This book is meant to help reduce the chances that you will forget something as it will act like a guide to direct you along the way to making all of the wise decisions that you need to make sure that you get right every step of the process.

Talking to experts will be a good place to begin as these people have experience in helping people just as yourself take an idea regardless of how small or big that it is and guiding them to take the concept from start to finish and all points in between. If you are not able to do this, then I will give you the next best thing and that is the advice that you need in all the steps along the path to getting your business up and running. This is as complete and comprehensive of a guide as you can find as I am sharing all of my secrets and tips for the first time with you. You may be asking yourself why I would do this. The answer is simple, I want you to succeed and to be as successful as I know you are capable of being.

The steps that will be laid out in front of you will bring the process of starting your own business to life and show you all of the things that you should be thinking about in order to make sure that your efforts to start a business will not be like so many others and end in a complete and disastrous failure.

There is always going to be some one that will see disaster long before it happens and as a result of this, they will be in the know as to how they can go and stop the disaster long before it happens. While still there will be those that simply are going to sit back and let things happen as they know that there is a certain course that things have to travel in order to make the best decisions in their business life. Taking the advice that is presented here will be the best move that you can make that will help a person to make a decision that is both wise as well as successful for them in the long run. Let's begin our journey into this sometimes tough topic to discuss.

CHAPTER ONE: COMING UP WITH YOUR IDEA

One of the most difficult steps for a person to get past, is that of making the decision as to what type of business that they are going to open. The reason for this is that these people either have no clue as to what type of business they want to go into or are not sure how their idea can be transformed into a business idea. This is why it is important that they need to take a few minutes and sit down and determine what it is that they want to do and how exactly they are going to go about it?

The first thing that you need to do is determine the industry that you are wanting to go into business. This industry will lead to a bigger and eventual decision that has to be made which is that of what section within this industry you will finally go into business. Before you go too far into this discussion, you need to ask yourself some serious questions that will hopefully lead you to making some discoveries on your own. Being able to answer these questions will in general help you to make a wise decision and lead you down the correct path to get a good business for yourself up and going.

Let's for a moment take a minute and look at a person that is really good at working on cars. The fact is that they can go into a number of different businesses that will give them the financial freedom to not have to worry about making a living. We will look at the things that a person going into this line of work might otherwise overlook in the process of getting their business up and going.

The first thing that you need to address is the question of is what you are thinking about doing something that you are good at and that you can do well? If the answer to this question is yes, then you are well on your way to finding a business idea that you can go into and make a good amount of money at doing. This however is not the only question that you need to ask, there is also the question that has to be asked in regards to **is** what you are thinking about doing something you love?

Often a person will go into a business based on the simple fact that the line of work is something that is popular to do. The fact of the matter is that this is the wrong reason to be going into this line of work. If you are not passionate about the potential business that you are looking at starting, then you are not going to make a success as your heart simply will not be in this type of work.

Is the type of work that you are looking at going into one that has a broad enough range that you can keep the business going year round? Many people will come up with an idea for a business that is based on a seasonal concept or one that will not have a long term range to sustain business for a long period of time. This reason will generally lead to a person going out of business in less time it took to set the business up. You need to make sure that you have a business idea that can hold on long after the initial interest has lowered some.

Does your idea have the potential to be sold at a price that will cover the expenses you incurred and still be able to give you a profit in the end? This question is one area that a number of people will struggle at in the fact that they will not have the ability to even cover their expenses to provide the product or service. The other issue is that if they do cover their incurred expenses, they don't have the ability to actually make a profit and are out of business in a short amount of time.

The last thing that you need to make sure that you cover is the fact of can you raise the funds needed to hold your business up until it becomes profitable? This area of the thought process gets a little murky as you will nine times out of ten have to be able to refer to the savings that you have in order to make a profit. You will need to make sure that your business has the capital needed to hold out through the tough times as well as the good times. In the process of getting funds, you need to figure out what your long term goals are and how much you will need to cover at least a year to two of expenses until you begin to make a real profit.

If you have been able to answer these questions, then you can move on to the next area of concentration and that is the area of what line of work are you looking to go into business? After you have managed to master these two questions, then you can begin the rest of the process of sitting down and actually putting into motion the roadmap that will become the thing that either leads you to full on success or complete and total disaster.

The next few chapters will be vital that you read and implement all of the advice that you will find in them. It is these chapters that will help you to reveal the road to riches that you are so desperately seeking out. There are a lot more options out there for starting a business than you might expect. The key is that you simply need to make sure that you are looking in the right areas to help and ensure that the right fit for you is found.

Assess the questions that were asked here and see for yourself if there is something that you can get into business with that you can actually be successful at? Often times the answer surprises people that I tell this to.

They will ask me how to decide what line of work that they should go into and I will tell them that they need to follow their heart and follow the things that they are good at to get the right fit for them and their new business needs.

Even after you have accomplished this task, the amount of work for you will have just begun and you will have a lot more that you will have to do even before your first customer has made their first purchase. The next chapters will lay this out starting with the process of building your business plan. This part of the process is very important as the business plan will be what gives investors an idea as to what your business will be about as well as the amount of money you need to request.

CHAPTER TWO: BUILDING YOUR BUSINESS PLAN

The business plan is one part of the process of getting up and going that has to be looked at closely. There are a lot of people that think that after they come up with an idea, it is just time to make things happen. This is in some regard true while other areas of this will mean that you have to take things in a more structured manner. Too many people make the mistake of trying to go from barely having an idea for their business to the first day of business. This leads often times than not to failure that happens on an epic level. The thing that needs to be looked at is that of the process to get any business regardless of its size up and running. The most crucial part of this process is that of the business plan. If you have a strong business plan, then your chances at success will be a lot better than if you have a plan that is weak as water. Too many people go to lenders with a business plan that deep down will not hold any real merit and won't have the elements that will get them the funds that they are wanting and needing. This chapter will discuss these things in great detail and help a person to see that their business plan is the foundation that their dreams will either be built upon or will be what leads to their dreams being destroyed.

Executive Summary

The first part that should be included in your business plan is that of the executive summary. This is a very important part of the business plan and gives the lender that you are trying to get funds from a brief and clear picture of the business and you as individuals. In business the one thing that will determine if an investor be it a bank or a private individual will look at is the executive summary. This one part can be what makes them decide to keep reading or what leads to them tossing it into the trash and dismissing you without a single penny being invested.

It is this importance that you need to be aware of and the reason why you need to make sure that this is giving your investor the best image possible. You need to help give the person reading the business plan a reason why they should want to continue to read in hopes that they will see what it is that you envision as well. If you are a business that has been established in the past, then this section will be a little easier to write as you have sections that you can fill out that a person who is new and never been in business can't fill out. If you are new, then you need to make sure even more that you are giving the best image possible for your business vision. If you have followed the advice of the earlier section and given the investor the information that they are looking for, then you will have a lot more success in building upon the next sections.

One thing that you can do is demonstrate the fact that you have a strong background and give a little insight as to that background along with the reasons that you made the decisions that you made in going into business. This can help to paint a picture to your potential investors as to who you are and what it is that drove you to make the decision to go into business.

Another thing that will help you in the fact that you are a new business is that you show the investor that you have done the market research that has been needed to be done to have an idea as to what is needed to open up and actually be successful in your business endeavor. The next section you will want to make sure that you include is that of the company description.

Company Description

This part of the business plan is vital as it also gain helps to paint a picture as to what your company is all about and how you are planning on taking the money that you are seeking out and how you plan on using it to get your business up and going. This is a second chance to better the impression that you make with the executive summary and enforce some of the points that you might not have got across in the process of the executive summary.

So what is it that needs to go into the company history portion of the plan? This is not a long list and if you know all the details to include, you can write this part of the plan in a very quick and effective manner. Talk about the nature of the business you are looking to start and how there is a need in the market that your business can serve in an effective manner. Go on to talk about how exactly your business will go about serving these needs and giving a person the service that they are hoping for.

Elaborate on the experience that you have that will set you apart from the rest in terms of trying to get your business up and going. An investor will be interested in the things that you consider to be your strong suits and see how exactly you are planning on making full use of these and how you plan on accomplishing this. This allows us to move on to the next section of the market analysis.

Market Analysis

In this section, this will be where you show your knowledge of the market as well as the industry on the whole. This is an ample example to show off that you have a good understanding of the data that you have gathered while talking about this industry. There are a few things that you need to make sure that you include in the market analysis to ensure that the person looking over the business plan knows that you understand what it is that you are presenting to them.

First start with an industry description as well as outlook to help and show that you have researched the industry you are looking to go into. Show that you know all aspects of the industry and that you can compete on any size level that you are required to do so. After this section will come the next of information that pertains to that of your target market. Make sure that you narrow your target down to a reasonable size. It is too often that a person will be overly ambitious and will try to conquer the large market on their own. This often will lead to a complete and total failure of the business and lead to them having to sit back and figure out what went wrong.

Looking at all aspects that are related to the world of your market can give your potential investors the information that they are seeking out to see in an effective business plan. If you demonstrate a serious lack of this knowledge, then you can be setting yourself up for some bad news in terms of getting the funds you seek to get your business up and running.

With that being dealt with, you can then write the next section of your business plan the details about the way that your company is organized and how it will be managed.

You will have some serious questions that you have to address when it comes to the people that will be running the business, what experience that they have and what their exact duties will be. Having this information to give to your potential investors will give them a clear image as to what experience that these people have and if they are in fact qualified enough to take on the duties that they will be assigned.

One area that many people make a misstep in is this section of the plan. They will not have a clear picture as to who will be involved, why they are experienced and what their exact duties will be. I have seen a number of people that have come to me and asked what it was that had went wrong in their business plan. I look at their plan and I see this one area that has some serious holes in it and I point this out to them. They often times will tell me that they did not realize that this information was as crucial as some of the other parts. I often tell them that every part of a business plan is crucial and that any one detail that is not dealt with in the proper manner has the potential to do a world of damage to their odds of getting a loan for their business.

I advise these people that they need to make sure that they go into this process with a clear vision as to what their structure will look like in terms of organization too often good business ideas go awry due to there simply not being a structure in place that will tell the investor the who's and what's of their business plan. Before we go any further, you need to stop and look at the people that will be in your business and see what it is that each of them will be doing and how these duties will be carried out on a regular basis.

Now that you have accomplished this very easy part of the plan, you need to now sit down and look at these people and list their experience and skills that make them qualified enough to perform each of the duties that they have been tasked with. For each person including yourself, you will need to make sure that you answer and address the following areas.

- Names of any and all of the owners of the company. Often a person will think that this information is simply not needed as a person may not be part of the immediate day to day operations. Regardless of how big of a part or small of a part that they do, you need to make sure that they are listed in the business plan in this section.

- Percentage of the ownership of the business that each person will have or currently already has. This will be crucial as an investor wants to see if the company is in dire straits, who will be responsible for the business.

- Extent of involvement with the business that these people will have on a day to day basis and how involved will they be in the exact operations?

- What are the forms of ownership that you and the other people will have in place? There are numerous types of ownership that you can choose to implement in the overall day to day operations of your business. Talk to your other partners and see what you feel will be the best for all parties involved. This has to be in place before you will get one penny from an investor as many people will not be willing to hand out money without a structure of partnership in place.

- Management Profiles for all of the people that will be involved in the business. You need to make sure that you put these people and their experience on display. Too many times this part of the ownership of the company is overlooked and the person will wonder why it is that they did not get the funding that they were seeking out. It is often a simple matter of the experience of these people were not on display.
- Taking these people and putting their best foot forward will generally help them a lot of times to get the needed funding that their business will need to get up and going. Including a detailed list of the persons experience will be just what they need to convince an investor that their business is a wise one to invest in. I have included a list of the things that needs to be listed concerning these people and their resume in terms of experience.
- Name

- Position that the person has held at prior jobs in the past. Even if you think that it is minor and not relevant to the position that they have with your business you need to list it to help and give the investor a better picture of the person in question.
- Primary responsibilities that the person had while employed at the business. This can be as major of a duty or as minor as sorting mail. Put all of the duties on display to help the person that you are asking for the money a better picture of the range of duties the person has had in the past.
- Education of the person. Include any relevant training that they have got in the course of their previous jobs. This can be anything from training to use a certain type of program to anything that is looked at as being relevant to the performing of their proposed jobs.
- Unique experience and skills that they have managed to acquire while in the process of doing their job. Many people look at these skills as being useless and thus don't always

include them in their work history, the simple fact of the matter is that every skill no matter how minor should be listed.

- Prior employment
- Special skills
- Past track record
- Industry recognition
- Community involvement
- Number of years with company
- Compensation basis and levels (make sure these are reasonable -- not too high or too low)
- Be sure you quantify achievements, doing this will give a better clear picture of the duties that you had and how well you were able to perform these duties. Listing this type of experience alone can have a very positive impact on the way that you will be viewed while in the process of performing your duties.

Services or Product Line

This is the part of the business plan that you get to pitch for a better term to potential investors the thing that you will be selling or the service that you will be performing. The person you are looking to invest in your business, needs to have a clear picture as to what it is exactly that you are looking to offer. If you have a product that you want to sell, you need to make sure that you include any and all relevant information on this product. If it is patented, you need to make sure that you include the patent in your materials as well as any documentation that you have that is related to the actual product.

If you are looking to sell a service, then this is where you need to make a strong pitch as to why you are qualified to do this as opposed to your competitors. I have had a number of people that have all finished their business plan, taken it to their lender and been told a flat out no in terms of their business plan for the simple fact that they have yet to tell the investors or convince them that they are qualified to provide the service that they are looking to provide.

This information is most of what you will need along with any and all relevant financial documents to include. The investor needs to know what you are bringing to the table in terms of your own money, what you are looking to do with the money and how much money will you need for your business. Even if you go low on your numbers, the lender may think that you are going too low and that you have no idea as to what you are actually doing. The next chapter will discuss the next steps you need to take in helping to get your business up and running.

CHAPTER THREE: CHOOSING YOUR BUSINESS STRUCTURE

Making a decision as to the type of business structure that you will go with will be a very important part of your decision making process. The reason that this is so crucial is that in all regards that you decide to go with, you will need to make sure that you provide the potential investor. There are six different types of business structure that you can use and before you proceed any further, you need to make the decision as to which one you are going to go with. This can be a part of the whole process that will be the most frustrating as you will seem to just want to give up and make a decision based out of desperation to get past this roadblock.

It is important that you make sure that you look at all aspects of this and ensure that you are going with the best structure that is right for your particular needs. We will look at all of these and hopefully after this has been done, you will have a better idea as to what direction that you will want to go in,

Sole Ownership

This is one of the more commonly used types of business structure and will be the one that the biggest selection of people will go with. This is as it sounds, you are the only one that is associated with the ownership of the business. A lot of times a person will think that this means that they are the only one that works at the business when in fact it is not the case. You can have a hundred employees that work for you, if you are the only one that has anything to do with the ownership, then you are considered to be a sole ownership situation.

Limited Liability Company

A person that makes the decision to go with an LLC will often have a lot of things that they need to make sure that they look at these steps are in place to ensure that you don't make any serious oversights in the process of the forming of the LLC. Too often a person will overlook the most minor of details and will in the end think that they have covered everything. While each and every state has different variations on this, it is important that you keep this basic structure in mind so that you have an idea as to how things are needing to go for you and your business structure. Understanding the things needed for a successful business structure will be crucial in helping to have an idea as to the organization of your business and how things should be structured.

You may decide to go with a partnership in terms of your ownership and getting all of the aspects in place. A partnership is one thing that you may want to think about in terms of getting going in the business world. The way that this can work is that two or more people will own a part of the company this will depend on the number of partners that you have as to how much of the company that each person will own. If t is a matter of two people, then the ownership is going to be broken down to around 50/50.

The two main types of partnerships is that of a couple of people going into business or four people going into the partnership and each person will own 25% of the company. You will want to do it this way as to prevent any one person from having all of the control and being in charge without the consent of the other partners. If the ownership is divided up evenly, then there is no chance of things not being equal.

These are a few of the things that you can think about when you are looking at the world of your business structure and making sure that you get the best results for you setting up your business. In the next chapter, we will discuss the things that you need to think about when it comes to the location of your business and how the location can make all the difference in the world as to your success or failure on the whole. All of the before mentioned chapters are useless unless you have a structure and a solid location that you can park your business at and help to get customers to come your way in a regular basis. Having the right location can make or break your business and lead to your ultimate success or your eventual ruin.

Chapter Four: Finding your Businesses Location

We hear it all the time, people talking about how the location of a business can make or break their overall success. It is a sad fact but the simple truth is that if you don't have the right location your business will never have the chance to reach its full potential. Knowing the things that will make or break this location can be crucial in making sure that you are not setting yourself up for disaster in the long run.

First you need to decide where you are going to do business. This means you need to decide are you working from home, buying a location or simply renting space. These answers will be the heart and soul of your decision making process. Having these answers will afford you the chance to go to the next step of this decision making process. If you are going to work from home, then you have taken a good portion of the process off of you, there is however some things that you still need to think about as well as things that you need to make sure that you are in compliance with in terms of local and state regulations.

One mistake that a person will make is that they think that if they are doing business from their home, it is simply a matter of just opening up for business and going to town, the truth of the matter is that you actually need to make sure that you are getting the permits as well as any other licenses that will be required by your city or state. This violation of the rules can cost you a load of money and send you to a point that you are having a lot more difficulty getting your business up and going. You also need to make sure that you are following any and all zoning regulations that will be in place. We will discuss that in greater detail in the next couple of sections.

Sometimes you're going to run into the issue that your business is not zoned properly. This can be an issue from you're in a zone that does not allow business to an issue with you being zoned for a particular type of business that you're not falling into. Often if you are found to not be working in the right zone de0ending on the severity of the violation, you can get a minor fine or in much worse cases, you can be shut down altogether. Taking a little time to understand the way that these regulations work will be crucial in helping you in the long run to avoid a lot of the mistakes that I have seen a lot of people make over the last several years.

You also need to look at the type of business that you are going to open and see is there a market that is in the immediate area for you to tap into? Many people think that just opening a business anywhere they choose will work when in fact that you will have to make your efforts that much more intense just to be in a position that you can actually get people to come in. things like a restaurant, or other type of food service will be able to function at almost any location unlike a person that wants to open a surfboard shop in a city that is nowhere near an ocean. Think about your business and see from there if you can actually succeed with it being where it is located or are you setting yourself up for disaster.

Talking to others that have been in the same situation will be very helpful in the fact that many people will learn from their mistakes and if you are willing to listen, will actually share their experiences with you and help to guide you from making the dame list of mistakes that they have made in the past. Talking this out and bouncing your ideas past them will generally help you to see the pit falls before you hit them and allow you to side step the issues and take your business workings to the next level. I have seen what can happen when you go into a business without half of the information that you are needing. This can lead to a disaster and in many cases will lead to you not being able to master your basic needs.

Once you have got all of the initial work done in terms of looking for a place that can be advantageous for your business, you will want to make sure that you then begin to actually look for a place that you can rent from or that you can buy to open your business in. if you have not done this part of the process, then now is a great time to begin the process and evaluate the good and bad things about a particular location. See what it will take to renovate it to fit your needs. Does is even come close to being useful for you or are you just using the place out of desperation to have somewhere that you can call home for your business? If you have answered this question along with done your homework, then you are really ready to call your new location home for your business. By the time you have managed to get all of the early work accomplished, you will feel like you have been on an uphill battle, but in the end, it will be a ride that is more than worth it and that will most of the time lead you feeling more than fulfilled for the most part.

The next chapter will deal with something that is a little more complicated of a thing to discuss and that is the actual financing of your business dreams. Knowing where and how to get financed will be the most important part of this entire endeavor. I will help you to see that there are a number of ways that you can help and get the funding that you are needing and wanting for your business.

Chapter Five: Getting your Dream Financed

Financing your dream business is something that is few times thought about at the early stages of a business getting up and going. The truth of the matter is that it is one of the most important things that you need to be thinking about as there is no dream to fulfill if you don't have the money you are needing to make your business actually succeed. There are a number of ways that you can take your hopes of a successful business and turn it into a reality if you know which of the many rocks to look under in terms of getting the funding that you are needing. This chapter will deal with the number of ways that you can get the funding that you are seeking out and help your dream not crash and burn like a number of the ones I have seen come to a sudden and tragic end most of the time.

Firs thing that you need to make sure that you do is to sit down and figure out the amount of money that you will need from your lender. This needs to be as close to an exact number as you can get, Figure out every single detail all the way down to the number of toothpicks you will need if opening a restaurant. Having this information will be crucial in helping you to master the funding issues you are coming up with. You will need to make sure that you sit down and take a careful look at all of your expenses to make sure that you don't underestimate the amount of money that you are needing to need just because you are not sure the exact number of things you will need.

I often will tell people I consult that they need to sit down and take a look at the number things that they will need and to write down these things on a regular basis. Then after they have done that, they need to determine as best that they can the exact number of these things that they will need. This will give them a ballpark number that they can begin with and work from there as to the total amount of money that they will need. I have had a lot of people come back after doing this and told me that doing that helped them a lot and led to them seeing the reason that their initial effort to get funding failed the way that it did. Lender will not want to loan you money if you are not even sure what the total you will need is and what it will be used for in the process of your business dealings.

After you have made this list, you now need to find a lender that will help you to achieve your goals. This can be a bit of a challenge as many people will not understand the many types of lenders that there. In terms of getting your funds you will need to know that there are a large number of loans that are open to you. One of the most common of these loans is that of a small business loan. A person that takes advantage of one of these loans will need to make sure that they have all their documentation and such in place so that they will not be turned down for not having everything as it should be.

There is a certain amount of time that will be involves with the repaying of these loans so you need to make sure that you know what the payment options are so you don't get caught off guard. Small business loans are an excellent thing that can help make your dream a reality

If you are looking for something a little more modern in terms of getting funded the use of crowd funding for getting the funds that you are needing for your business funding. The way that this generally will work is that a person will use some sort of service that specializes in crowd funding and allow you to post a project that you are looking to raise funds for. Investors then come across your project and will donate a certain amount of money in return for a service or other often that you can offer these investors. This helps them to feel that they are getting something in return for their donation.

These are just two of the things that you can use in helping to increase the odds that your bus9ness will get funded. While there are many other methods, these are along with a loan from a bank the main uses of banks are for people that have a set business plan in place and are looking to get a sizeable amount of money from the bank for their business.

Once you have mastered this part of the process, you can then head to the next section that is important and that is the process of hiring employees that will be a vital part in the process of getting your business up and going with the least amount of trouble. We will discuss this section in more detail in the next chapter. It is important though that the subject of dealing with finances be discussed before we talk about the employees that will be a vital part of your business.

Chapter Six: Hiring your Employees

The hiring of employees is one section that many people that are looking to have employees will need to make sure that they look at carefully before you just make an empty decision based on what your gut tells you. The truth of the matter is that you need to follow more than your gut and you actually need to make sure that you follow these simple yet very important guidelines in getting the right fit in terms of employees for your business.

First look at the positions that you need to have filled. This will give you an idea as to what your important areas are and the ones that can simply wait a little bit. The more important positions are the ones that you need to make sure that you fill first and work your way down from there. We will in the next few sections look at the things that you need to consider before you hire a single person to come in and work for your company.

First what is their experience in the past? There are a lot of employees that are just entering the working world and don't have any relevant experience. This does not mean that they don't make a good fit, this just is an area that you may want to hire them for areas that are not as important until they can get the training and experience to be promoted to other areas of the business.

You also need to make sure that you are informed if your potential employees are convicted felons or have issues that you need to know about this is not an automatic disqualification for you to hire a certain employee, it is however something that you need to make sure that you are aware of and are able to work around if need be. Another thing that you need to make sure that you are aware of is their ability to work in the country legally. You will need to make sure that you fill out all the needed documentation for them to work in this country. You will also need to make sure that you have them fill out all of the needed tax information for them to be able to work in the United States. This will help you to make sure that you are not getting into trouble with the government and are well within compliance.

You will have a million things that you will need to accomplish in order to get your business up and running. The last of these is the thing of having to sit and talk to potential employees. It is for this reason that you hire a person that you have a lot of trust in that you can sit down and have them do all of the interviewing for you. This will take a lot of responsibility off of you and free you up to be able to focus on a lot more important things.

You need to make sure that you cover as to if you are going to provide benefits to your employees and if so are they going to be regular employees or part time ones or all employees. This is a very important decision that you will need to make sure that you make before you begin the process of hiring an employee as many of these employees will want to know if you offer any type of benefits package and if so what is it and how competitive is it to others that are in the same industry?

This will be a very important part of the process as you may find a perfect qualified employee and they may not want to work with you as you don't offer them any type of benefits. The other thing that you need to make sure that you cover when talking about hiring an employee, is the level of experience that they have. This is a very important part of the whole process that should be looked at closely in helping you to determine if a person will be a good fit for your job or not. After you have made the decisions as to who you are going to hire and those that you are not going to hire. It will be easier to simply wait and get the right fit for your job as opposed to trying to replace people until you find the right fit for your position. This will be a very important decision that you have to take serious and ensure that you are taking the needed steps to get the best employees for your business.

Chapter Seven: Location, Location, Location

The location of your business can make or break your business efforts and lead you to the point that you will either feast or starve. Talking to others that have made their location bad decisions, I have seen a lot of people that have all went the way of closing their doors simply because they opened their business and the customers did not come like they had been promised they would. I give these people the same advice and hope that they will take it and lead them to the promised land of being successful I am offer you this advice for a fraction of the price that I would normally offer to people and that is free.

Finding a place that is right for you and your business will be vital in helping to ensure that you are not looking at an empty business due to a lack of people coming in and doing business with you. If you are a restaurant, then you need to make sure that you go and locate yourself to a place that is centered around a shopping center will be vital in helping you to ensure that you are getting the best chances at customers coming into your business. This would be an example of taking a golden opportunity and making the most of it.

If you are a restaurant and you are not following this piece of advice, then you can be setting yourself up for failure and never even be thinking about it. I had a client a few years ago that made this very rookie of a mistake and did not open their business up in the right part of the city. They suffered for some time before coming to me and asking for my help.

I asked them a few basic questions and soon determined that the problem with their business was all based on the issue of that of location. I saw that they were not tapping into the market that they had and were letting their competition take all of their business from them. I advised them to close their current location or to simply try and open a new location in a part of the city that was a little friendlier towards them

If you were for example looking to open a surf shop, then you would want to make sure that it is located near a body of water. A landlocked location will not sell as much as one that is less than a mile from the ocean. This is the one example that I give a lot of my clients when they come to me and ask for my advice as to what they need to do. I give them the surfboard example and most times they see where I am trying to go with it and understand the meaning of what I am saying.

Being in the wrong place will most times hurt your odds of being noticed and attracting either new customers or keeping the ones that you have. I have seen a lot of great concepts that a person had go up in smoke due to the simple fact that they did not think about their location before opening the doors of their business.

Another thing that needs to be expected to consider about the location of your business is that of talking about the amount of work that you will have to do on the location you are thinking about. Often a person will find a building that is perfect for them and will generally not think about the large amount of work that will be required to make the building perfect for them to start their business in.

If you find a business that was there that you have to put a ton of effort into to make it a reliable place to open a business in, then you will generally find yourself in a situation that you will put more money into the location than you really should. In other words, don't try open a surfboard shop in a business that used to be a restaurant as you will have to put a load of work into the building and may actually hurt your chances at actually making a real profit with your business idea.

Talk to the realtor and see if there are any other locations that they have that may fit your needs a little better than the one you are currently looking at. They often will have something that is either not officially listed or something that they just had listed that may be right for you and your business needs.

Chapter Eight: Opening day

All of your efforts have come to this one point, it is time to actually open your doors to your business. You can be in a hurry and simply open up and let the people find you, or you can do things the right way and actually find the people to come to your business. In one word success will come down to one word, marketing.

Marketing your business is crucial in the fact that you have to find the people that you will be doing business with. A lot of the people that are looking for a place to do business with will make their decision based on the marketing that is placed in front of them. This n turn means that you have to make sure that you are getting the word out in an effective manner and one that will make a person want to come and do business with you.

Look at the things that makes your business one of a kind and unique. This should be taken into consideration and placed in the marketing that you will be doing for your business. There are a number of companies that you can get to do your marketing for you and you will need to make sure that you pick one that will give you top of the line results for the money that you are looking to invest in your business.

One thing that I suggest for my clients is that they will run a special for their new clients that come to them. People love deals that seem like they are getting something for nothing and this as a result means that if you are running a deal that will give them a special deal, then you are giving the customer your best effort. Taking into consideration what your overall message will be that you are wanting to portray to your potential clients. Many people will overthink this and as a result will generally see that their efforts are not being as effective as they could be if they had hired a marketing firm to handle their marketing.

Opening specials are one of the most popular things that a number of businesses will run in hopes of getting the attention of their potential customers. Talking about these specials, you need to ask the people that are in charge of your marketing what if any ideas do they have. It is vital that you listen to them and take all of their advice to see your business have a successful opening. Often times I will have people come to me and tell me that they could have been more successful if they had success in their first few weeks of operation. I ask these people what if anything did they do that would have driven sales to their establishment and they generally will tell me that they did not do anything at all. I see this happen more and more on a regular basis and in the end have to tell these clients that they made a huge mistake by letting their business fail and not taking advantage of the opportunities that were in front of them.

Chapter Nine: After the celebration has ended

In business, there will be a period of time that you will experience a lull. This is known as the cool off period. This is something that happens to almost any and all businesses on a regular basis. This is why when talking to you about the business plan, I suggested that you make sure that you have money for when you have a lull in the amount of business that you are doing. Too many people think that this is a myth that will never happen to them, but it will. Talking to a marketing specialist will generally help you to see that your goals are not over realistic. The people with the marketing firm will be able to guide you as to what you need to do in an effort to ensure that your lull time will not be as hard on your business as it could possibly have been.

There is more to your overall success and long lasting success than the cool off period. You will need to have a long range plan that will be in place that will ensure that your initial momentum will be successful and that your odds of failing will be greatly reduced. I ask a person that comes in to have me help them what is their five year plan. I am amazed at how many of these people that have no idea as to what their plan is for the next five years. They all tell me that they have simply been focused on dealing with the area that is right in front of them.

I tell these people that if they have any hopes of making a success of their business, then they will need to make sure that they are following the advice that I give them. Often they will follow this advice, and other times, they will simply act like they are the ones that knows what they are doing and that my advice is more of a distraction to them as opposed to being actually helpful for them. I look at them and at that moment, I know that they are quickly going down the road of ruin and that without any real assistance, their hopes and dreams of being in business for a long time will come to a crashing end.

Having a long term plan in place will help any person to be prepared for the if that will come along in life and help them to actually survive the hardest of times that will be put in front of them. Having a plan will lead to them knowing the ins and outs of being a successful business owner as opposed to simply just getting by or being another statistic.

CONCLUSION

As you are able to see, there are a lot of things that need to be done in the process of helping a person even if they are skilled in opening up a business to see the many advantages that can come from taking a little time to review the information that is listed here and putting it to use ion the course of opening a business. While it will be quite an endeavor and seem like it is too much from time to time, you will want and need to take this guide as a step by step instruction to getting your business up and going. Not every business owner will succeed and not every one of them will automatically fail. The key is to reads the information in this book and use it in your life to see the path that you need to take to have a very positive outcome for the most part.

As business is only as good as the person that is behind it, this in turn means that if you are willing to take the needed time to learn a few of these proven steps, then you will soon be in a position to take your efforts to the next level. Few business owners will actually heed this guidance and will try to be one man against the world. This type of effort will generally lead to them failing in a grand and glorious fashion. If they know a little about the way that a business can go from a small idea in your head all the way to a much larger and more successful business venture.

Success is always a reflection of the amount of effort that you put into it. If you are looking to make an impression in the world, then you need to think success and believe that in your heart, you have as good of a chance at success as any other person. The more that you think this, then the greater your odds are that you will be fully successful in all things that you do in your life.

www.ingramcontent.com/pod-product-compliance
Lightning Source LLC
Chambersburg PA
CBHW071820170526
45167CB00003B/1378